Diesterwegs Neusprachliche Arbeitsmittel Englisch

Herbert Bodenschatz

Text-Analysis

Kombinierte Textaufgaben für Grund- und Leistungskurse

Verlag Moritz Diesterweg
Frankfurt am Main · Berlin · München

ISBN 3-425-04120-7

Gesamtherstellung: Druckerei Haßmüller, Frankfurt am Main 56

Inhaltsverzeichnis

Vorwort

Die vorliegende Sammlung von Textaufgaben orientiert sich an den Forderungen, wie sie den Prüfungsvorschlägen der Kollegstufe in den meisten Bundesländern zugrundeliegen. Um das sprachliche Spektrum des Schülers vor allem im Hinblick auf das Abitur zu erweitern, ist es nötig, im Unterricht zusätzlich zur schwerpunktmäßigen Behandlung von Einzelthemen bzw. Kursmodellen eine möglichst breitgefächerte Sammlung nichtfiktionaler Texte zur Verfügung zu haben. Die bewußt gewählte inhaltliche Verschiedenheit der vorliegenden Texte bedingt zugleich eine starke Variation in Wortschatz und Idiomatik, wobei als dominierende Textsorte gehobener Journalismus vertreten ist. Dabei wurde darauf geachtet, britische und amerikanische Publikationen gleichermaßen heranzuziehen.
Bei der Textauswahl standen folgende Aspekte im Vordergrund: Erstens wurden Texte mit gestuftem sprachlichem Schwierigkeitsgrad aufgenommen, die das wirklich aktuelle Gegenwartsenglisch dokumentieren. Zweitens war darauf zu achten, daß zwar möglichst moderne Themen gewählt wurden, aber nur solche, die über das unmittelbare Tagesgeschehen hinausreichen.
Um die Sammlung für Grund- und Leistungskurse zugänglich zu machen, enthält sie einfachere und kürzere sowie schwierigere und längere Texte. Von den Arbeitsaufgaben her sind jedoch alle Texte in beiden Kursen verwendbar.
Die Fragen gliedern sich in zwei Bereiche (*Questions on the text* mit Fragen zu Inhalt, Aufbau, Sprache, Stil, Intention des Autors und *Composition* mit Themenvorschlägen für Essays u. ä.). Auf direkte sprachpraktische Übungen wie pattern drills und dergleichen wurde verzichtet, da diese im englischen Abitur in einer solchen Form nicht vertreten sind. Ebenso wurden keine bestimmten Zeilen zum Übersetzen angegeben, da sich die meisten Textpassagen auch für diese Übungsform eignen und da der einzelne Lehrer nicht in der Auswahl ihm geeignet erscheinender Stellen eingeengt werden sollte.
Da die Bewertungsschemata in den Bundesländern differieren, wurde auf die Beigabe eines Punkteschlüssels verzichtet. Dafür ist für die Textaufgabe Nr. 8 im Anhang ein Lösungsmuster beigefügt, das als Einführung in den Bearbeitungsmodus und als erste Hilfestellung für den Schüler zu verstehen ist.

Herbert Bodenschatz

1 The gentleman and his club

All gentlemen belong to a good club. They do so for a number of reasons, many of which are unconnected with what an outsider might consider to be a club's main purpose — a sociable meeting place. In fact, clubs are very often not sociable places at all. For example, there was the case of the elderly member of one of the most exclusive of all clubs who complained most bitterly to the Secretary: "D'ye know," he said, "there was a demned young fellow I have never met, who came up to me in the hall and said 'Good morning'!" "Good gracious," said the Secretary, who must be all things to all members, "whatever did you say?" "Well," said the old member reasonably enough, "I did not want to appear rude so I just turned my back and walked away."

Another reason for a gentleman joining a club may be because his father and his grandfather belonged to it before him. More likely it is because he finds it a convenient place to have parcels sent or messages taken or for the equally practical reason that it is the one place where he is not expected to tip.

Most of the traditional clubs have changed little with the passing of the years largely because of the innate conservatism of the members. Many years ago there was a great brouhaha when the Athenaeum went so far as to install a lift to enable the more elderly to use the facilities of the club above ground level. Unfortunately the proportions of the new lift were almost exactly as if it had been designed to accomodate a coffin standing on end, which enabled the younger members to remark that its real purpose was to facilitate the removal of such ancient members as had died in the bedrooms.

(Incidentally it was the Athenaeum where the late Lord Birkenhead used to stop off to relieve himself on his daily walk from his home to the House of Lords. When challenged, after adopting this practice for some time, as to whether he was a member, he was supposed to have exclaimed: "Good God, is this place a club as well?")

There are now, however, signs in some of the less distinguished clubs that the conservatism and carefully erected barriers are slowly being broken down. Some clubs in an effort to increase the revenue have even allowed clubmen to bring their wives or lady friends to dine in certain remote rooms on specified nights of the week. As, as someone has rightly remarked, most clubs have the atmosphere of a Duke's house with the Duke lying dead upstairs, it is not a move which has been unanimously approved of by the ladies, who prefer a little more glitter on their evenings out. To add to their discomfort the premises set aside for the use of ladies are often adapted from some remote and unused billiards room or, certainly in one case, an over-large lavatory, which makes the ladies' attitude even more understandable.

The advantages which gentlemen's clubs used to have in such matters, for example, as members being able to drink and gamble long after establishments open to the general public were closed for the night have largely been eroded by the changing laws which have resulted in a rash of late night rendezvous to which membership is open to almost anyone who cares to apply.

This may be part of the cause for the recent concern amongst gentlemen's clubs over falling membership. Traditionally they have always been more concerned with whom they should exclude rather than with whom they should admit. Now, as many are cautiously opening the doors wider, they are finding with some chagrin that there are not queues of would-be gentlemen clamouring for admission. Just the same, there are still enough good clubs where gentlemen who wish to preserve the traditional barriers can do so and where it is still advisable for a member to put his son's name down at birth. In these the port still circulates after dinner and members can amuse themselves, as one of them put it, by sitting at the window and "watching the demned people getting wet outside".

650 words

Douglas Sutherland in
The English Gentleman,
London, 1978.

Annotations

3 **sociable** friendly — 7 **demned** slang form of 'damned' — 19 **innate** possessed from birth — 20 **brouhaha** / 'bru:ha:ha: / (colloq.) fuss, excitement — 25 **to facilitate** to make easy — 28 **to relieve oneself** to use the toilet — 32 **distinguished** famous — 40 **premises** the building(s), offices where a business is carried on — 47 **to erode** to destroy gradually — 47 **rash** a sudden breaking out — 54 **chagrin** / 'ʃægrin / anger

I. Questions on the text

1. What are the reasons for joining a club? How do the members and the author see this?
2. What does the author do to enliven his text?
3. Which examples does the writer give to show that even clubs must move with the times?

4. Why do you think could clubs of this kind survive so pertinaciously in England?
5. How does the club system reflect certain aspects of English society?
6. Try to characterize the writer's style. Give examples.
7. What is meant by the expression "clubs are very often no *sociable* places at all?" (line 5)
8. Explain the meaning of the words in italics:
   a) one of the most *exclusive* clubs (line 6)
   b) they prefer a little more *glitter* (line 39)
   c) *would-be* gentlemen (line 54)

II. Composition

Write about one of the following subjects in about 150—200 words.
1. Do you think that clubs as described in this essay are still justified today? Try to find pros and cons.
2. Give an (ironical) description of the 'typical gentleman.'
3. a) For boys: You want to join a gentlemen's club and write a letter of application to the management. (You can satirize the letter if you like.)
   b) For girls: You are a lady and want admission to a gentlemen's club. Write a letter to the management, giving arguments for your wish. (You can also satirize if you like.)

2 Tourists in London: tour force

The question seems to be: do we want the tourists or do we not? Probably only in London, and there only in parts of London, are we aware of them as a pervasive and inescapable presence, locusts, monopolising the West End, jamming the public transport, disputing in absurd languages, spreading vast maps on the sidewalks; we have tourists like Los Angeles has smog.

They drift around with a purposeful aimlessness; they make life exasperating for the natives who inhabit a city that is a penance to live in anyhow. The tourists are said to be an export asset. They contribute to the balance of payments, whatever they are: therefore everyone who is shoved off the pavement into the busroutes of Oxford Street is contributing to the national exchequer. Or so they say.

The other day the playwright John Osborne, once the standard Angry

Young Man and apparently fossilised in that ageing role, did a vehemently bitter and I would say rather ill-mannered piece in our local evening paper, recommending us Londoners to go out of our way to make life so disagreeable and unpleasant for the tourists that they will get fed up with us and go away. Snub them, said Mr Osborne, insult them, misdirect them, pretend not to understand their language, overcharge them — treat the tourists, in short, the way British visitors are treated in Paris, just to teach them a lesson not to come back.

That seems to me an overreaction. Tourists get in my hair as much as they do in Mr Osborne's, but I have a residual conscience about them. I have spent so much of my life as a professional alien in almost every country that I feel an intuitive sympathy for anyone brooding over a street map at a troublesome corner, with no proper words to ask the way. I am fundamentally friendly. When a tourist accosts me at Euston and asks how to take the Tube to, say, Acton Green, I escort him (knowing nothing about it myself) to the Underground map and show him. I never ask why on earth he should want to go to Acton Green.

I am not always fundamentally friendly. Only a couple of days ago in Portland Place I was tapped on the shoulder in a most peremptory way; naturally I assumed it was the CID catching up with me at last. Not so; it was a German in a tartan jacket.

"Hyde Park," he said, "Where is?"

I paused to collect my thoughts as to how you got from Portland Place to Hyde Park, and this seemed to annoy him. "Hyde Park!" he snapped, "Is here?" and pointed directly at the BBC's Broadcasting House.

"Correct," I replied, nettled. "In there, take the lift to the sixth floor, and there you will find Hyde Park."

John Osborne would have been proud of me.

I must be becoming unpleasantly insular. I grumble at rich Arabs, I also grumble at evidently non-rich and inoffensive young Scandinavians crowding the Unterground, bearing vast burdens on their backs, each one occupying as much room as two working commuters. Where, I wonder, do they put up all those tents and sleeping-bags and field-kitchens that they ceaselessly manipulate round Piccadilly and Bond Street? Do they in fact ever put them up at all? Or are they just the insignia of the new European wandervogel forever travelling hopefully, never to arrive? Except, perhaps, at Acton Green.

Or maybe the sixth floor of Broadcasting House.

630 words

James Cameron in *The Guardian*
(World and Press Oct. 1978).

Annotations

1 **tour force** here: mass tourism; also allusion to 'tour de force' = feat of strength — 3 **locust** / 'ləukəst / Heuschrecke — 8 **exasperating** irritating — 9 **penance** punishment — 10 **asset** valuable or useful quality — 10 **balance of payments** G. Handelsbilanz — 13 **Exchequer** Government department in charge of the nation's finances — 14 **Angry Young Man** 'Angry Young Men' was a term given to a group of British playwrights and novelists of the 1950's, who manifest hostility toward existing traditions. — 15 **fossilised** out-of-date or antiquated — 17 **to go out of one's way** to try hard — 23 **to get in one's hair** to get on one's neves — 28 **to accost** to address — 33 **peremptory** (too) commanding, insisting on obedience — 34 **CID** Criminal Investigation Department — 35 **taran** Scottish woollen fabric woven with coloured crossing stripes — 40 **nettled** angry, irritated — 46 **commuter** person who travels regularly by train or car between his work in a town and his home in the country or suburbs — 49 **insignia** symbols

I. Questions on the text

1. How has the author organized his text?
2. What form does James Cameron use for his text and why?
3. What is the relation between John Osborne and the writer of this text?
4. What's your opinion of John Osborne's 'advice'?
5. Why can it be said that tourists make life exasperating for the "natives"?
6. Find examples of irony in the text.
7. What does the incident with the German tourist show?
8. What are the wider implications of his behaviour and of Osborne's 'advice'?
9. Paraphrase the following expressions. Do not use the words in italics.
   a) a *pervasive* and *inescapable* presence (line 4)
   b) *monopolising* the West End (line 4)
   c) *overcharge* them (line 20)
10. Explain:
    a) they drift around with a purposeful aimlessness (line 8)
    b) I have a residual conscience about them (line 24)
    c) I must be becoming unpleasantly insular (line 43)

II. Composition

Write about one of the following topics in about 200 words.

1. In a letter to an English newspaper complain about the treatment you have got as a tourist in Britain. (You can also write about positive experiences, if you prefer.)

2. An English friend writes you a letter and complains about bad treatment he has received as a tourist in Germany. Send him a reply.
3. Why do people travel abroad?
4. Try to show the clichés about the 'typical' German abroad or the 'typical' Englishman resp. American in Germany. What is your personal opinion regarding such stereotypes?

3 Art of the hamburger

Ray Kroc is a small, energetic 75-year-old, as unpretentious as hamburger, as salty as French fries, as American as frozen apple pie. He is worth upwards of half a billion dollars, which is not bad for a man who started his business when he was 52, and whose most expensive product costs less than a dollar.

Kroc was a salesman with boundless enthusiasm for his products, especially the Multimixer, a machine for mixing five milkshakes simultaneously. Selling had taken him into a zillion restaurant kitchens by the time, in 1954, he heard that two brothers were using eight Multimixers at their quick-service restaurant in San Bernardino, Calif. He went west to investigate, and like Cortez starting at the Pacific, looked on with a wild surmise. He got the right to franchise what he saw, including the brothers' name and the golden arches. In 1955, he opened his first McDonald's in Des Plaines, Ill., and began grinding it out.

Today, McDonald's ranks first among retailing companies in terms of net income. This year, McDonald's will open its 5000th store. It has sold 25 billion hamburgers, and is selling a billion every three months. Twenty-five billion hamburgers would make twenty piles the size of the world's tallest building, Chicago's Sears Tower. The flour for 25 billion buns would make 5 feet of powder on the ski slopes of Aspen and Vail. McDonald's has sold enough shakes to fill every gas tank in America.

The earth must slope before a river can flow, and the public must be predisposed before a success on the scale of McDonald's can happen. The Second World War got many American palates accustomed to standardized fare, from C rations and from factory canteens. Europeans linger over meals; Americans regard food as fuel to be taken on the way steam locomotives took on water, scooping at full speed from troughs between the rails. This vast and polyglot nation has never pretended to have a national cuisine. Americans generally want food that is hygienic, copious and fast.

Kroc did not just launch a company, he energized an industry. The fast-food industry — $ 14 billion a year — is one reason why one of every three American meals is eaten out. Kroc has been called the "service sector's equivalent of Henry Ford."

Franchising is a solution to the problem of distributing goods in a continental nation. Automobiles, gasoline, motels, fast food: many franchised products are for mobile people who value familiarity because they want to feel at home away from home. Franchised products are part of the homogenizing of experience that a nation of travelers finds more reassuring than boring.

Kroc's enterprise expresses the prosaic idea on which American prosperity rests: things add up. Enough billions of fractions of anything add up to a lot of something. Obsessive attention to detail — to boxes of buns, to time-and-motion studies — pays because America is the realm of mass effects. Like many entrepreneurs, Kroc's genius is for acting on the obvious, or what seems obvious after he has acted on it.

680 words

George F. Will in *Newsweek*
(World and Press, April 1978).

Annotations

2 **unpretentious** modest, not trying to seem important — 9 **zillion** innumerable; an indeterminately large number — 13 **surmise** here: imagination — 13 **to franchise** to get the right to market a company's goods exclusively — 15 **to grind it out** to produce — 16 **retailing company** Einzelhandelsgesellschaft — 18 **billion** Brit. Billion, Am. Milliarde — 21 **Aspen and Vail** famous ski resorts in Colorado — 26 **C ration** iron ration (for American troops in the Second World War) — 28 **to scoop** schöpfen, schaufeln — 28 **trough** / trɔf / long open box for animals to feed or drink from — 29 **polyglot** knowing, using many languages — 30 **cuisine** style of cooking — 31 **copious** existing in large amounts — 40 **to homogenize** make similar or identical — 45 **time-and-motion study** study in rationalizing — 45 **realm** / relm / kingdom, region — 46 **entrepreneur** / əntrəprə'nə: / Unternehmer.

I. Questions on the text

1. How has the author organized his text?
2. Compare the first and last paragraphs in terms of language and contents.
3. Sum up the main facts of Kroc's career.
4. What is the secret of Kroc's success story?

5. To what extent is it typical of the American way of life resp. social system?
6. Which particular device does the author use to illustrate the enormousness of the McDonald's enterprise? Give examples taken from the text.
7. What are the reasons that fast-food restaurants could become so popular in the United States?
8. Why do Americans regard uniformity as an advantage?
9. Explain:
   a) as unpretentious as hamburger (line 2)
   b) the public must be predisposed (line 23)
   c) polyglot nation (line 29)

II. Composition

Choose one of the following topics and write about 200 words:
1. Fast-food restaurant are a decline of culture. Comment critically on this statement.
2. Americans regard food as "fuel to be taken on the way". What do you think about that?
3. Why do you think are McDonald's restaurants so popular with many young Germans?
4. Describe your experiences with foreign food during your holidays abroad.

4 Delirium of disco

The pace is fast, as never before. The beat is literally a gallop. The dancers swing and spin like lindy hoppers, but they slide, clasp and strut with the suave grace and loose hips of Latin lovers. They're supposed to touch, but it's only touch and go. The dancing may not bring cardiac arrest, but it makes for restless nights, hung-over days and a persistent feeling that you can't clear your head of that maddening ta-ta-tum. The name of this latest epidemic of the dancing sickness is disco.

You don't need a thermometer to tell there's a fever. There are now more than 10,000 discotheques in the U.S.; last year no less than 37 million Americans got out on the disco floor at least once. The total revenues of that first big season of operation were in excess of four billion dollars — equivalent to two-thirds of the combined gross income of both the recording and movie industries. A glance at the Billboard charts showed that four of the top 10 records in the nation were disco songs and that a large proportion of the entire top-40 list was either disco music or music that showed the influence of its beat and style. As the second great season progresses, disco is being packaged and franchised like McDonald's, with new places opening at the phenomenal rate of 20 per week. A sign of the immense profitability of the new industry is the price tag on these dance halls. The current trend is toward lavish and immensely costly installations that rival the old movie palaces of the thirties and cost up to three million dollars. There is plenty of action every night as disco becomes America's foremost form of live entertainment and participatory culture. No contemporary recreation has so perfectly blended all the elements of the new society of the seventies. In an age when physical appearance and conditioning have become obsessively important, disco provides a perfect arena for the exercise and display of all those carefully nurtured and cultivated bodies. Most important, just when a whole new generation of young people are coming to maturity, eager to assert themselves on a stage as emblematic of their world as were the rock concerts and be-ins of the sixties for their older brothers and sisters, disco provides a fresh focus for a leisure life. At the same time, for most kids it is a far more exciting and challenging opportunity than anything that they are likely to find in the real world.

Far from being the kind of mass leveling that rock was, the disco world mirrors everywhere the principle of social segregation. People want to party with their own crowd and keep the strangers out.

Studio 54 in New York City is the epicenter of the social whirlwind, the greatest discotheque in the world. Of course you don't just go to Studio 54, you make elaborate preparations for the event. In a world where everything turns on appearances, the first step is to make sure that you are properly clothed. The disco world prides itself on being totally liberated from all the old dress codes. The disco chics make their selection from a wardrobe that is either virtually empty or a costume closet that contains enough disguises to outfit a professional spy.

Studio 54 is a private club. It's so exclusive that it often bars its own members. The secret of its enormous success is precisely its capricious and outrageous snobbism. The result is that the mob outside the door on a Saturday night appears to surpass in numbers and frenzy the crowd in Times Square on New Year's eve. All night long the club's proprietor stands at the desperately besieged door, flanked by his elegant maitre d'street and his team of manmountain muscle, picking and choosing, barring and losing the thousands of people who submit themselves to the terrible trauma of rejection.

The profits that can be earned in a big-time disco operation are enormous.

The greatest attraction, the music, costs the management virtually nothing. The records are provided free by the record companies in the hope that the disc jockies will "break" the new releases and precondition the public to buy the albums when they appear a month later in the stores. What's more, the canned music is infinitely superior to what can be provided by a live band.

Modern music is so completely a product of the recording studio that even the famous rock bands can provide only a crude approximation of their familiar hits when performing before an audience. The disco sound is vastly more elaborate than rock and completely artificial. A highly contrived, supersophisticated electronic artifact, disco is precisely the kind of pop music toward which history has been driving since the first player piano. A totally eclectic style, compounded equally from the most primitive and backward-looking and the most advanced and futuristic sounds of our day, disco owes just as much to the conservatory as it does to the ghetto, or the jungles of Africa and South America. Only in an age of total access, of cultural pluralism, of a commercial opportunism that thinks of everything and stops at nothing, could you have such an extraordinary product.

Why apart from the love of fun, has disco got everybody in such a lather? The simplest answer is to examine its underlying myth, which was exposed in Saturday Night Fever. When you examine the picture, you discern a contemporary version of the lonely, self-involved adolescent or young adult hero represented in movies of the 1950s by James Dean, Marlon Brando or Montgomery Clift.

Saturday Night Fever was a shot heard round the world. It spoke to the condition of millions of well-dressed, physically beautiful boys and girls who have everything — and nothing. Modern youths are still lonely, but they're not seeking love. They have found it — in their own reflections.

1000 words Albert Goldmann in *Life*, November 1978.

Annotations

3 **lindy** making jerky movements — 3 **to strut** to walk in a stiff, selfsatisfied way — 4 **suave** smooth and gracious in manner — 5 **touch and go** here: lasting for a short time only — 5 **cardiac arrest** stoppage of the heartbeat — 11 **revenue** income — 13 **gross income** / grəus / Bruttoeinkommen, Bruttoeinkünfte — 14 **Billboard** big American musical magazine — 14 **chart** hit parade — 18 **to franchise** to sell the goods produced by a particular factory — 20 **price tag** label (for showing prices) fastened to a product — 21 **lavish** giving or produc-

ing freely — 24 **participatory** / pə'tisipətəri / providing the opportunity for individual participation — 31 **emblematic** serving as a symbol of s. th. — 31 **be-in** a gathering of hippies — 32 **focus** Brennpunkt — 39 **epicenter** part of the earth's centre, above the origin of an earthquake — 39 **whirlwind** Wirbelwind — 48 **capricious** guided by caprice — 50 **frenzy** madness — 52 **to besiege** to surround a place (with armed forces) — 52 **maitre d'street** / 'metrə də stri:t / word formation analogous to maitre d'hotel = chief waiter — 59 **to precondition** to influence in advance — 61 **canned music** music on records (in contrast to live bands) — 66 **to contrive** to invent, design — 67 **artifact** artificial product — 68 **player piano** a piano containing a mechanical piano player — 69 **eclectic** choosing freely from various sources — 81 **lather** / a: / here: an agitated state

I. Questions on the text

1. How has the author organized his text?
2. Characterize in short the introductory passage.
3. Summarize the main facts about disco music as given in the text.
4. What are the economic aspects of discos?
5. Why does the author pick out the example of Studio 54?
6. Why — according to the author — are people so enthusiastic about discos?
7. Why can it be said that no "contemporary recreation has so perfectly blended all the elements of the new society of the seventies"?
8. In the title the author uses the word *delirium*. Where else in his article can you find expressions that are related to this term? Interpret them in short.
9. Why can discos be compared to McDonald's?
10. Explain:
    a) a stage as emblematic of their world (line 31)
    b) the epicenter of the social whirlwind (line 39)
    c) disco music owes just as much to the conservatory as it does to the ghetto, or the jungles of Africa and South America (line 71)
    d) an age of total access, of cultural pluralism (line 73)
11. Do you agree with the author's conclusion in the final passage?

II. Composition

Choose one of the following topics. Write about 200 words.

1. What is your own view on discos and disco music?
2. A newspaper has published a review of a pop concert. You disagree with the article and write a letter to the editor.

3. a) A friend of yours, an ardent lover of classical music, vehemently denies that disco music has any value at all. Write him a letter and try to modify his opinion.
b) A friend of yours who is an absolute disco fan has never been to a classical concert. Try to persuade him to go with you to such a performance.

5 The latest teen drug

Her first drink was Scotch and Coke, and then she started guzzling anything that would make her high. She soon became a heavy boozer, a party girl and a pill freak. When she finally moved in with her boyfriend, she drank, watched soap operas and became so paranoid that she dreamed of throwing herself onto the subway tracks and had urges to crash her head through plate-glass store windows. To deal with her bouts of depression, she had to force herself to make verbal no-suicide contracts with several friends. When she reached that point, Carrie was 18 years old and had been drinking for five years.

Taking a drink is virtually a rite of passage for adolescents in this country, but while kids once drank for kicks and because it seemed cool, alarming numbers now frankly set out to stupefy themselves. "We're seeing a growing number of kids who are alienated and using alcohol to escape from other problems," explains Loran Archer, acting director of the National Institute on Alcohol Abuse and Alcoholism (NIAAA) in Washington. "And if they are starting younger they are more likely to get into heavy drinking in later life." Indeed, teenage drinking is perceived to be such a problem that millions of dollars are being allocated for counseling and prevention programs and the alcoholic beverage industry itself is starting to sponsor alcohol awareness ads.

Who are the young problem drinkers? "The group with the highest risk of having future alcohol problems are children of alcoholics," explains NIAAA's Archer. "Whether it's environmental or hereditary, alcohol problems seem to run in families." The highest proportion of drinkers are youngsters from upper-income families, but the rate of abuse is greatest among young American Indians. The lowest proportion of heavy drinkers is found among young blacks, even though in later years they have a far higher death rate than whites from cirrhosis of the liver.

The reasons why teenagers abuse alcohol are myriad. Peer pressure is still a strong factor. "The kids who drank seemed to have something I wanted," says a 20-year-old recovered alcoholic from Kansas who took her first drink at 13. "I didn't know what it was. All I know is that I never felt I belonged anywhere." She deliberately sought out the heavy drinkers, dropouts and drug dealers. "I felt close to them," she explains. "Our common aim was self-pity."

More recent studies suggest that even though the peer group may provide an encouraging setting, it is the parents who are the stronger influence.

The increase in adolescent alcohol abuse is also symptomatic of the stress and permissiveness of the times. "Escape through drugs," quips one 19-year-old member of Alcoholics Anonymous. "It's the American way." And there is the naïveté of many well-meaning parents, who, during the drug scare of recent years, have pushed alcohol as a safer alternative to other substances.

"Young people are more aware than adults that alcohol is a drug," explains Joe Weisenberger, an AA adviser in Indianapolis. "But they do not see themselves as skid-row types and so their greatest barrier to treatment is denial."

Prevention programs are difficult to evaluate, the impact of alcohol education is hard to measure and nobody is certain it is working.

"Everything that we are doing is to some degree an act of faith," says Donald Light, director of Alcohol Programs for California's San Mateo County Department of Health and Welfare. "When you talk about preventing alcohol abuse, you are talking about eliminating human suffering. Social programs just cannot eliminate it all." True enough. But that only throws the problem back to the family — and that's where it started in the first place.

650 words

Newsweek, January 8, 1979.

Annotations

2 to guzzle to drink greedily or habitually — **3 high** stimulated by drugs or alcohol — **3 boozer** drinker — **4 freak** / i: / a drug addict; a person who has broken away from conventional society — **5 soap opera** a television serial which is usually about the characters' private troubles — **5 paranoid** / 'pærənɔid / a person suffering from a lasting disease of the mind, believing that others are purposely mistreating and hating him — **7 bout** an attack of illness — **11 rites of passage** ceremonies which celebrate an individual's or a group's transition from one status to another within society — **12 kicks** thrill — **13 to stupefy** to surprise very much; to make unable to think — **14 to alienate** entfremden — **19 to allocate** to give — **21 to sponsor** to pay for a commercial radio or TV programme in return for advertising of products — 29 **cirrhosis of the liver** / si'rəusis / Leberzirrhose — 30 **myriad** / 'miriəd / a great and varied number — 30 **peer pressure** pressure of peer groups — **peer** belonging to the same group in society — 34 **deliberate** done on purpose — 35 **dropout** a person who drops out of school or ordinary society and tries to practise another life-style — 40 **permissive** allowing a great deal of, or too much, freedom — 40 **to quip** to make a witty remark — 41 **Alcoholics Anonymous** (AA) American organization for the prevention of alcoholism — 43 **scare** state of widespread fear — 46 **AA** = **Alcoholics Anonymous** — 47 **skid-row** a poor dirty part of town where unemployed and alcoholic people gather — 48 **denial** here: refusal

I. Questions on the text

1. How has the writer organized his article?
2. a) Characterize the introduction.
   b) Why did the author choose this particular form?
3. Sum up the reasons why young people take to drinking.
4. To what extent are parents responsible for the alcoholism of teenage boys and girls?
5. Why can it be said that the increase in adolescent alcohol abuse is symptomatic of our times?
6. The author quotes several people in his article.
   a) Sum up what they say.
   b) What is the function of these quotations?
7. Try to analyse the style of this article.
8. Explain:
   a) the industry is starting alcohol awareness ads (line 21)
   b) the greatest barrier to treatment is denial (line 47)

II. Composition

Choose one of the following topics. Write about 150 words.
1. Alcohol — a drug like others? Give a critical comment.
2. Write a letter to the editor, complaining about the fact that drinking is being stimulated by advertising, films and TV.
3. Drinking should be forbidden as well as smoking. What do you think?

6 The frustrations of British feminists

A judge recently ruled that a Fleet Street bar called El Vino was simply being chivalrous in prohibiting women from standing at the bar with men. They can drink at tables in the rear without being jostled, he said, so El Vino's rule does not violate the Sex Discrimination Act. The ruling caused a brief outburst from militant feminists, but in the larger public it caused more jocularity than outrage. One feminist said it was unfortunately true that many British women don't care about that sort of thing and rather like having drinks bought for them by chivalrous males.

Britain, the birthplace of the 19th century feminist movement, has celebrated the 50th anniversary of women's full suffrage. But 50 years of voting have not brought equality. Britain's vigorous women's liberation movement lists dozen of ways in which women are still a class apart. Women's earnings are only 65 percent as high as men's and, after a period of sharp gains, seem to have leveled off in the race to catch up. Women seldom appear on company boards and in the top executive ranks.

The income tax law treats women like children. A husband is responsible for filling out his wife's tax return, making it impossible for her to hide any of her income from him. On the other hand, a survey a few years ago found that 7 out of 10 British wives did not know how much their husbands earned.

Women are forced to retire from work at age 60, men at 65.

For all the obstacles in tradition and law, British women have made considerable progress in recent years. Some believe that the women's movement in Britain is now more aggressive and cohesive than the American one that inspired it.

The movement's most significant legal gain in recent times was passage of the Sex Discrimination Act by Parliament in 1975. It went into effect simultaneously with a previously passed Equal Pay Act. Before the discrimination act, the young woman who took El Vino to court for refusing her service at the bar would have had no legal grounds for complaint. In spite of the El Vino setback, which many believe will be overturned on appeal, the act has opened many male strongholds to women. Even the notoriously men-only preserves, private clubs, have mostly opened their memberships to women, if only in restricted ways and just in time for the new members to see the clubs driven out of existence by economic and demographic changes.

British women, who make up 40 percent of the nation's work force, tend to be more interested in economic discrimination than other sex-related issues. There is deep resentment over imbalances in pay that remain in spite of the equal pay law, which mandates that women be paid wages equal to those paid to men who do similar work.

Many British women, reared to think of themselves as dependent, do not aspire to more responsible jobs. Girls do as well as boys in all academic subjects, but only small numbers try to get into male-dominated professions such as science and engineering.

Even those who try often find their way blocked by custom and institutional rigidity.

The frustrations of British feminists were pointed up in a recent court case from Sheffield. A publican refused to let a young woman play snooker in his pub, saying women ripped the table's covering with their cue sticks. The woman took him to court and won. But when she went back to the pub, he threw her out again — for swearing. She reportedly is trying to decide whether to take him to court again.

560 words

The New York Times,
(World and Press, Oct. 1978).

Annotations

2 **Fleet Street** street in London with the offices of many newspapers — 3 **chivalrous** / 'ʃivəlrəs / being polite and helpful (especially to women) — 4 **to jostle** to push — 5 **Sex Discrimination Act** law against the unequal treatment of women — 7 **jocularity** amusement — 11 **suffrage** right of voting in political elections — 25 **cohesive** tending to stick together — 33 **appeal** Berufung(sverhandlung) — 33 **stronghold** place where an idea has strong support — 34 **notorious** widely known for s.th. bad — 34 **preserve** something considered to belong to a limited number of people — 37 **demographic** illustrating conditions of life in a community — 43 **to rear** to bring up, to educate — 44 **to aspire** to be filled with ambition; to desire strongly — 48 **rigidity** stiffness, inflexibility — 50 **publican** owner of a pub — 51 **snooker** game played with balls on a billiard-table.

I. Questions on the text

1. Sum up the facts connected with the El Vino trial.
2. Which changes were brought about by the two acts against the discrimination of women?
3. How and where are women being discriminated in British society?
4. Why is it remarkable that women have to suffer from these disadvantages in Britain?

5. How would you characterize the judge of the El Vino trial?
6. How would you characterize the behaviour of the publican in Sheffield?
7. Why do British women seldom get into responsible male-dominated professions?
8. Why can it be said that the El Vino trial has opened many male strongholds to women?
9. What difficulties has the British women's liberation movement to fight with?
10. Explain:
    a) El Vino was simply being chivalrous (lines 2—3)
    b) which . . . will be overturned on appeal lines 32—33)
    c) demographic changes (line 37)

II. Composition

Choose one of the following topics. Write about 200 words.
1. A man defended the decision in the El Vino trial in a letter to the local newspaper. Write a letter of reply in which you criticize his attitude. (You can use a very emotional tone.)
2. Total emancipation is against the real interests of women. Comment critically on this statement.
3. Why are women being discriminated in our society?

7 Detectives' lives – fact and fantasy

Real policemen, both in Britain and the United States, hardly recognise any resemblance between their lives and what they see on TV — if they ever get home in time. There are similarities, of course, but the cops don't think much of them.

The first difference is that a policeman's real life revolves round the law. Most of his training is in criminal law. He has to know exactly what actions are crimes and what evidence can be used to prove them in court. He has to know nearly as much law as a professional lawyer, and what is more, he has to apply it on his feet, in the dark and rain, running down an alley after someone he wants to talk to.

Little of his time is spent in chatting to scantily-clad ladies or in dramatic confrontations with desperate criminals. He will spend most of his working life typing millions of words on thousands of forms about hundreds of sad, unimportant people who are guilty — or not — of stupid, petty crimes. Most television crime drama is about finding the criminal: as soon as he's arrested, the story is over. In real life, finding criminals is seldom much of a problem. Except in very serious cases like murders and terrorist attacks — where failure to produce results reflects on the standing of the police — little effort is spent on searching. The police have an elaborate machinery which eventually shows up most wanted men.

Having made an arrest, a detective really starts to work. He has to prove his case in court and to do that he often has to gather a lot of different evidence. Much of this has to be given by people who don't want to get involved in a court case. So, as well as being overworked, a detective has to be out at all hours of the day and night interviewing his witnesses and persuading them, usually against their own best interests, to help him.

A third big difference between the drama detective and the real one is the unpleasant moral twilight in which the real one lives. Detectives are subject to two opposing pressures: first, as members of a police force they always have to behave with absolute legality; secondly, as expensive public servants they have to get results. They can hardly ever do both. Most of the time some of them have to break the rules in small ways.

If the detective has to deceive the world, the world often deceives him. Hardly anyone he meets tells him the truth. And this separation the detective feels between himself and the rest of the world is deepened by the simplemindedness — as he sees it — of citizens, social workers, doctors, law-makers, and judges, who instead of stamping out crime punish the criminals less severely in the hope that this will make them reform. The result, detectives feel, is that nine-tenths of their work is re-catching people who should have stayed behind bars. This makes them rather cynical.

460 words

"Detectives' lives — fact and fantasy"

Annotations

4 **cop** slang for policeman — 12 **scantily-clad** almost undressed — 14 **form** Formular — 15 **petty** unimportant, small — 25 **court case** examination in a law court before a judge — 26 **witness** person who gives evidence under oath in a law court — 41 **behind bars** in prison

I. Questions on the text

1. Sum up the main differences between detectives in real life and detectives on TV.
2. Why is most television crime drama centred around finding the criminal?
3. Why do TV productions show detectives different than they are in reality?
4. What makes a detective's work particularly difficult?
5. Why must a detective know nearly as much law as a professional lawyer?
6. Why do detectives become cynical?
7. Explain:
   a) his real life revolves round the law (line 6)
   b) to stay behind bars (line 41)
8. What is meant by "elaborate machinery" (lines 20—21)? Try to give concrete examples.
9. Why don't people want to get involved in a court case?
10. Why does hardly anyone tell a detective the truth?

II. Composition

Chose one of the following topics. Write about 200 words.
1. Describe a famous TV detective you know.
2. Why do people like TV crime dramas?
3. Take the standpoint of a disillusioned policeman and write a letter to the editor, critically examining the "simple-mindedness" of law-makers.

8 Dracula lives

He is our most enduring monster, an aristocrat of evil who sates himself on human blood and climbs into his ancient coffin to sleep the dreamless sleep of the undead. He is cursed with immortality; only the rays of the sun, or a stake through his heart, can end his sanguine quest. He has died a thousand deaths — on stages, screens and television, in comics, novels and stories — and still his lethal glamour persists, as deathless as our love of horror — and our fear of death.
"Good evening, I am Count Dracula." Fifty years ago, an unknown

Hungarian actor named Bela Lugosi stepped out onstage at New York's Fulton theatre, and his deep sepulchral greeting has never been forgotten.

A myth as potent as Dracula's doesn't spring from one mind alone. Though Bram Stoker's novel first appeared in 1897, vampires have been with us, a part of our collective unconscious, since the ancient Egyptians. The Greeks called them vrykolakas, and even today in the wilder parts of Greece animals are locked up at the time of a funeral — lest they walk over the corpse and prevent the dead from sleeping in his grave.

There was a real Dracula, one Vlad Tepes, or Vlad the Impaler, a fifteenth-century Wallachian prince (nicknamed Dracula, meaning "son of the devil", or "son of the dragon"). Vlad was no vampire, but he had a definite taste for blood. Defending his land against the invading Turks, he was noted for his tortures — impalement being his favorite — and on one infamous day massacred 30,000 people. Tourists to modern Roumania are taken to Castle Bran, where Vlad once took refuge; though it was not the real Dracula's home, it eerily resembles the Castle Dracula of the novel.

Vampires proved ideal for the screen, with its genius for metamorphosis, the phantasmagoric and the violent.

Like the vampire, movies are both fixed in time and immortal. If Dracula never grows old, neither will Bela Lugosi in the role, framed in what Leonard Wolf calls "the infinitely stopped moment." There have been more than 200 vampire movies made around the world, from F. W. Murnau's classic silent "Nosferatu" to Andy Warhol's "Dracula", which shows the vampire a junkie who can only get off on a fix of virgin's blood. But it's Lugosi, in Tod Browning's 1931 "Dracula", who retains the crown as king of the vampires. "I am Dracula": the words were never spoken with such definitive solemnity, and they haunted him throughout his career, confining him almost exclusively to ghoulish roles. Lugosi's drug addiction, which lasted for seventeen years, began during the filming of "Dracula", when he had to take morphine for the pain in his legs. From the time he played the Count, he was the prisoner of his blood stream. When Lugosi died in 1956, he was buried in his Dracula cape, white tie and tails. After the services, Peter Lorre and Boris Karloff approached the open coffin. "Boris," said Lorre, "do you think we should drive a stake through his heart?"

What is the hold Dracula has on our imaginations! Horror, of course, can be fun, a great escape that transmutes our amorphous anxieties into simple black-and-white conflicts. But horror tales take us back to ourselves as well, reminding our bodies with a rush of adrenalin that we are alive and want to stay that way. Dracula offers the promise of everlasting life — and everlasting death. Of all fiends that haunt our popular mythology, he is the most richly ambiguous and perhaps the most relevant to our American dreams — to our fear of death and our fixation on the ideal of infinitely prolonged youth. Enfolding his victims in his long black cloak, he is the overprotective mother who never lets go of her children, the stern patriarch who protects his tribe from extinction. Transfixing virgins with his gaze, he is the lover who liberates our carnal passions. In his latest incarnations, he has become a more romantic, alluring figure than we had imagined. He still scares us, but he tempts us, too. He is both Faust and Mephistopheles, our demon and our dream. He is us. Dracula lives.

720 words

Newsweek, 1978.

Annotations

2 to sate oneself to satisfy oneself — 5 **stake** pointed piece of wood — 5 **sanguine quest** search for blood — 7 **lethal** / 'li:θəl / deadly — 11 **sepulchral** / si'pʌlkrəl / like a grave — 18 **to impale** to run a sharp stick through someone's body — 22 **impalement** (see above note) — 23 **infamous** wicked, shameful — 25 **eerie** / 'iəri / causing fear — 27 **metamorphosis** / metə'mɔ:fəsis / complete change from one form to another — 28 **phantasmagoric** / fæntæzmə'gɔrik / ghostly, dreamlike — 34 **junkie** drug addict — 34 **to get off** to experience the effects of a drug — 34 **fix** injection of a narcotic — 38 **ghoulish** / 'gu:liʃ / devilish — 43 **Peter Lorre** and **Boris Karloff** were famous actors in many horror films — 47 **amorphous** formless — 49 **adrenalin** / ə'drenəlin / a hormone made by the body during anger or fear — 51 **fiend** very wicked or cruel person — 52 **ambiguous** / æm'bigjuəs / uncertain; of doubtful meaning — 56 **stern** strict — 56 **extinction** destruction — 56 **to transfix** to pierce through — 57 **carnal** sexual — 58 **incarnation** a person or thing that is the perfect example of a certain quality — 60 **demon** / di:mən /

I. Questions on the text

1. How does the author structure his article?
2. How is the introductory passage to be interpreted in terms of style?
3. What is the connection between the historical Dracula and the fictitious monster?
4. How is the Dracula myth commercially exploited?
5. Why is Dracula so popular in film?
6. What influence had the film role on Lugosi's life?
7. What does the remark of Karloff and Lorre in line 44 say about these two actors and about Lugosi?

8. What — according to the author — is the effect horror tales have on people's minds?
9. To what extent is the title of this article justified?
10. Paraphrase the following expressions without using the words in italics:
    a) still his *lethal glamour persists* (line 7)
    b) a great escape that *transmutes* our *amorphous* anxieties (line 47)

II. Composition

Write about one of the following topics in about 150 — 200 words.
1. Why do so many people like horror movies? Give arguments.
2. Violence in horror movies and violence in westerns or whodunits — are they the same? Write a critical comment.
3. Write a letter to an American or British friend who is keen on horror movies. You disagree with him on that point and give him an ironical reply.

9 Is anybody out there?

The resurgence of public interest in UFOs — brought on largely by the popularity of two science,fiction movies, "Star Wars" and "Close Encounters of the Third Kind" — leads to one inescapable conclusion: we earthlings are as fascinated as ever with the romantic notion that "we are not alone" in the universe. Like H. G. Wells, we are intrigued at the prospect that intelligent beings from our or other galaxies may be trying to establish contact.

The National Aeronautics and Space Administration has told the White House that opening a new government probe of unidentified flying objects now would be "wasteful and probably unproductive" because of the absence of physical or tangible evidence for analysis. But despite NASA's reluctance to continue pursuing UFOs, its no-nonsense experts and many other reputable scientists have come to believe the prospects of intelligent beings existing elsewhere in the universe are very good. NASA, in fact, has just concluded a two-year scientific study with the recommendation that the United States start an ongoing search for extra-terrestrial intelligence.

Scientists already have made sporadic attempts to search for any incoming messages from distant worlds, but not on a continuing, systematic basis.

The SETI (Search for Extraterrestrial Intelligence) proposal is a modest one by NASA standards and would cost less than $ 1 million. It would not require installation of expensive new equipment at the outset but would primarily entail using new technology for analyzing radiation data already being received on existing antennas.

The NASA SETI report, the work of 15 reputable scientists aided by numerous other specialists, is the first official government study to recommend such a search and, as such, could prove to be a milestone in man's continuing attempts to expand his horizons and break the physical and mental fetters that have bound him to earth.

NASA officials stress that they are not proposing two-way communications. Since any civilization capable of sending such transmissions is apt to be light-years away, it might take two or three lifespans to reply to any "hello" picked up from outer space. But even if a systematic search eventually proves we earthlings are, after all, alone, the byproducts of the search in new technological developments would add greatly to our knowledge of the physical universe — just as the spinoffs from moonprobes have produced miniature computers and other innovations beneficial to earth.

"Were we to locate but a single extra-terrestrial signal," the NASA report notes, "we would know immediately one great truth: that it is possible for a civilization to maintain an advanced technology and not destroy itself. We might even learn that life and intelligence pervade the universe."

Likelihood of the SETI proposal winning approval is good, depending in part on the budget restrictions President Carter places on NASA in fiscal year 1979. Renewed public interest in the whole question of extraterrestrial intelligence may prompt Congress to insist that we keep our lines open for any really long long-distance calls.

560 words

The Christian Science Monitor,
(World and Press February, 1978).

Annotations

2 **resurgence** coming back to activity — 2 **UFO** Unidentified Flying Object; flying saucer — 6 **Herbert George Wells** British novelist (1866—1946) who, among other Utopian stories, wrote "The War of the Worlds" in which an invasion from Mars is described — 6 **to intrigue** / in'tri:g / to fascinate — 13 **reluctance** unwillingness — 19 **sporadic** happening irregularly — 30 **fetter** chain — 37 **spinoff** byproduct — 47 **prompt** cause

I. Questions on the text

1. Summarize the scientific items as given in the text.
2. It may be said that NASA's view on extraterrestrial life is to a certain degree inconsistent. Why?
3. Why is there renewed public interest in the question of extraterrestrial intelligence?
4. Why have scientists made only sporadic attempts to search for messages from distant worlds?
5. What technical difficulties in getting contact with aliens has NASA to face?
6. Why would it be interesting for science and useful for mankind to establish contact with extraterrestrials?
7. Paraphrase the following passages. Do not use the italicized words.
   a) ... its *no-nonsense* experts and many other *reputable* scientists (line 13)
   b) It would not *require* installation of expensive new equipment at the *outset* but would *primarily entail* using new technology (lines 22—24)
   c) *Were* we to *locate but* a single *extra-terrestrial* signal ... (line 40)
8. What is two-way communication?
9. Where does the author use a stylistic pun? Explain the expression connected with it.

II. Composition

Choose one of the following topics. Write about 150—200 words.
1. Give a critical evaluation of a science fiction film or story that you know.
2. Many people say they have seen flying saucers. What do you think about that?
3. Write a critical letter to your Congressman. You may complain that either too much or too little money is spent on space research. Give arguments.

10 What is school for?

I'm tired — and have been for quite a while. In fact, I think I can pinpoint the exact minute at which I first felt the weariness begin. I had been teaching for three years at a community college. I had, for quite a while, overlooked ignorance, dismissed arrogance, championed fairness, emphasized motivation, boosted egos and tolerated laziness. I was, in short, the classic modern educator.

One day a student, Marylou Simmons, dropped by my office. She had not completed a single assignment and had missed perhaps 50 per cent of her classes. Her writing, what little I saw of it, was illogical, grammatically incorrect and sloppy. "Can I help you, Marylou?" I said cheerily, ever the understanding and forgiving teacher. Her lip began to tremble; her eyes grew teary. It seemed she had been having trouble with her boyfriend. "I'm sorry, but what can I do?" I asked. Suddenly all business, Marylou said, "Since I've been so unhappy, I thought you might want to just give me a D or an Incomplete on the course." She smiled encouragingly, even confidently. That's when the weariness set in, the moment at which I turned into a flaming conservative in matters educational. Whatever Marylou's troubles, I suddenly saw that I was not the cause, nor was I about to be the solution.

When I read about the "functional illiteracy" of our students, the namby-pamby courses, the army of child psychologists, reading aides, educational liaisons, starry-eyed administrators and bungling fools who people our school systems, my heart sinks. Public schools abide mediocre students; put 18-year-olds, who can't decide what to wear in the morning, into independent study programs; excuse every absence under the sun, and counsel, counsel, counsel. A youngster in my own school system got into a knife fight and was expelled — for one week, I noticed in the paper that bus drivers regularly see riders smoking marijuana and drinking wine on the bus at, for God's sake, 8 in the morning. I could go on, but the public knows well enough the effects of a system of education gone awry.

Consider for a moment what caused the mess. A few years ago people began demanding their rights. Fair enough. They wanted equal education under the law. I'm for it. Social consciousness was born. Right on. Now, enter the big wrong turn, the one that sent our schools into never-never land. We suddenly, naïvely, believed that by offering equal opportunities we could make everybody happy, make everybody well-adjusted, forgive everybody who failed, and expect gratitude to boot. When students were surly, uncooperative, whiny and apathetic, educators decided they themselves didn't know how to teach. So they made it easier on the poor, disadvantaged victims of broken homes, the misfits, the unloved. Well and good. But the catch to such lofty theories is evident. Poverty, ignorance and just plain orneriness will always abound. We look for every reason in the world for the declining test scores of our children, except for stupidity and laziness.

I'm perfectly aware that I sound like an old curmudgeon and it frightens me more than it offends you. But I have accepted what educators can't seem to face. The function of schools, their first and primary obligation, is not to probe tender psyches, to feed and clothe the homeless, nor to be the papa and mama a kid never had. The job is to teach. The teacher's job is to know his subject, inside out, backward, forward and every which way. Nothing unnerves a student more than to have a teacher who doesn't know his or her stuff. Incompetence they cannot abide. Neither can I.

Before educators lost their way and tried to diversify by getting into the business of molding human beings, a teacher was, ideally, someone who knew a certain body of information and conveyed it.

I want them back, those fearsome, awe-inspiring experts. I want them back because they knew what a school was for and didn't waste any time getting on with the task at hand. They were hard, even at times unjust, but when they were through, we knew those multiplication tables blindfolded with both trembling hands tied behind our backs.

Before the schoolmasters and the administrators change, they will have to shake off the guilt, the simpering, apologetic smiles and the Freudian theories. Which is crueler? Flunking a kid who has flunked or passing a kid who has flunked? Which teaches more about the realities of life? Which, in fact, shows more respect for the child as a human being?

The young people are interested, I think, in taking their knocks, just as adults must take theirs. Students deserve a fair chance, and, failing to take advantage of that chance, a straightforward dismissal. It has been said that government must guarantee equal opportunity, not equal results. I like that. Through the theoretical fog that has clouded our perceptions and blanketed our minds, we know what is equitable and right. Mother put it another way. She always said, "Life is real; life is earnest."

Incidentally, she taught me Latin and never gave me air in a jug. I had to breathe on my own. So do we all.

925 words

Suzanne Britt Jordan in *Newsweek*, (World and Press, March 1978).

The author is college teacher in Raleigh, North Carolina

Annotations

2 to pinpoint to find — **5 to dismiss** put away from the mind — **5 to champion** to support — **6 to boost** to strengthen — **9 assignment** homework — **11 sloppy** careless — **16 D** is an American mark at school, meaning 'sufficient' — **Incom-**

plete is a notice in a school report, indicating frequent absenteeism of a student — 21 **illiteracy** / i'litərəsi / having little skill in reading or writing — 21 **namby-pamby** foolishly sentimental; lacking in character or substance — 23 **starry-eyed** impracticable, dreamy — 23 **bungling fools** stupid persons who do their job badly — 24 **mediore** / mi:di'əukə / not very good — 31 **to go awry** / ə'rai / to go wrong — 32 **mess** confusion, trouble — 38 **to boot** in addition — 39 **surly** / 'sə:li / seeming angry — 39 **whiny** plaintive — 41 **misfit** person who does not fit well into his social surroundings — 42 **catch** a hidden or awkward difficulty — 42 **lofty** high; proud, arrogant — 43 **orneriness** obstinacy — 44 **scores** results — 46 **curmudgeon** / kə:'mʌdʒən / a bad-tempered old person — 49 **to probe** to examine — 49 **psyche** / 'saiki / soul — 53 **to abide** to tolerate — 54 **to diversify** to vary — 55 **to mold** to form — 57 **awe** feeling of respect mixed with fear — 63 **simpering** artificial; assumed — 63 **Freudian** / ʃrɔidjən / relating to Sigmund Freud, founder of psychoanalysis — 64 **to flunk** to fail in an examination; to give a failing grade to a student — 72 **to blanket** to cover — 72 **equitable** fair and just — 73 quotation taken from *A Psalm of Life* by H. W. Longfellow — 74 **air in a jug** something useless; words without substance

I. Question on the text

1. How does the author structure the text?
2. What is Suzanne Jordan's present attitude towards students?
3. Why did she change her mind?
4. What — according to the author — should be a teacher's most prominent quality?
5. What — according to the author — is most students' attitude towards school?
6. Sum up the negative facts the author gives on students and the (American) school system.
7. How — according to the author — will a teacher best prepare a student for life?
8. To what extent are the facts reported by Suzanne Jordan applicable to the German school system?
9. Characterize in short the "classic modern educator" (line 6) and the "flaming conservative" (line 18) as understood by Suzanne Jordan.
10. What is the writer's intention in this article?
11. a) What stylistic means does she use?
    b) What is their intended effect?
12. Try to characterize Suzanne Jordan's mode of writing in one sentence.
13. Paraphrase the following sentences. Do not use the italicized words.
    a) a system of education *gone awry* (line 31)
    b) their first and *primary* obligation is not to *probe tender psyches* (lines 48—49)

c) the theoretical fog that has *clouded* our *perceptions* and *blanketed* our minds (lines 71—72)

14. How is the sentence "she never gave me air in a jug" (line 74) to be interpreted?

II. Composition

Choose one of the following subjects. Write about 200 words.

1. What is your personal answer to the title question?
2. Write a letter to the author, either supporting or opposing her views. Try to use a rather emotional style.
3. Make up an interview for a school magazine in which a student is asked his own experiences in the present school system. Try to find pros and cons.

11 Texas – the superstate

It was the state America loved to hate. Nothing more than a left turn on the way to California, a god-awful won't-it-ever-end stretch of monotony that seemed to tax the endurance of the coast-bound motorist. It was the state that killed the Prince of Camelot and replaced him with a crudity of its own. A raw and artless place, the home of loud and vulgar people who were richer than the rest of us and constantly rubbing it in, but who still propped muddy boots on the tablecloth. "People were always treating Texas like an ugly old woman," says an oilman from Odessa. "Everybody knows it's there, but nobody gives a damn."

If the state had any value at all to a condescending America, aside from its unfair abundance of natural resources, it was a dusty, wind-blown shrine to the true grit myth of the frontier. About the only thing Texans and the rest of America ever agreed on was the fact that Texas was different. It still is. But after decades of insecure braggadocio, tall tales and youthful excesses, that state of the Union and state of mind called Texas has turned into an economic superstate and a cultural comer.

The most visible and dramatic sign of Texas's sprint to greatness has been the sheer growth of the place, the prosperity and sense of well-being that sweep over it like the wind. Texas is the geographic and economic heart of the American Sun Belt, that recently recognized crescent that runs from the tidewater of Virginia to the sands of southern California. The Sun Belt now contains 51 per cent of the nation's people and a rapidly growing proportion of its business as the flight continues from the deteriorating cities of the North and East. And in this rush to the sun, Texas has reaped an influx of people and industry not seen anywhere since the golden boom in California in the two decades following World War II.

As California's golden era has topped out, Texas's has begun. Since 1960, the state's population has jumped by more than 25 per cent, to 12.5 million — third only to California and New York. Houston, the ultimate boom town, growing at better than 1,000 people a week, is now the fifth largest city in America. Dallas, the unabashed apostle of conservatism, is eighth, and San Antonio — despite its mañana philosophy — is tenth. Fueling it all is the spectacular explosion of oil and natural-gas prices in the past years — an unencompassable bonanza to the region that contains a quarter of the nation's oil and 35 per cent of its natural gas.

One way to measure Texas's importance as a state is to look at it as if it were still an independent country — as it was from 1836 to 1845. In gross national product, it would rank ninth in the free world — ahead of Brazil, Australia and Sweden — and in per capita GNP, it would be third — behind only the U.S. and Sweden.

Rising population, of course, creates its own growing demand for goods and services, but beyond that is the larger truth that Texas is more hospitable to business than any other state in the Union.

In a state so geared to production and old-fashioned entrepreneurial go-go, the price of general prosperity is borne by the industrial world's traditional losers — menials, the jobless, the unschooled poor. Fully a fifth of the state's 12.5 million people survive at or below the poverty line — among the ten worst such records in the nation. Texas ranks 39th among the states in per capita spending for social welfare — a result partly of the constitutional limit of a dollar a year per citizen for welfare, partly of Texas's rugged but heedless individualism. "We ain't gonna reward those who won't work," says one unreconstructed state representative. "That's not the kind of philosophy that made Texas great." In a TV commercial for a company that makes oil-field machinery, the perky young woman grins into the camera and says, "If you don't have an oil well . . . git one!"

But Texas, the new superstate, is so flushed with success and growth that few people find time to worry. It is true that growth has its limits and that all empires, from Rome to Los Angeles, eventually topple. And as the London Economist has commented: "The greater danger will come when Texas again alters its state of mind, when the vigor, imagination and pride of first-generation money gives way to the trust-fund wealth of a spoilt third generation . . . when the veneer of being and thinking Texan has grown thinner." But in the meantime, like all pilgrims on the eve of a new beginning in a new land, Texans believe that they have the ability and the resources to make it different this time — and to make it last.

990 words *Newsweek*, December 1977.

Annotations

4 **to tax** to strain — 5 **Camelot** / 'kæmilɔt / the site of King Arthur's palace in Arthurian legend; figuratively used for a time, place or atmosphere of idyllic happiness; the Prince of Camelot is an allusion to the assassination of President Kennedy in Dallas — 5 **crudity** roughness — 10 **nobody gives a damn** slang for: nobody cares — 11 **condescending** behaving graciously, but in a way that shows one's feeling of superiority — 13 **true-grit** true — 15 **braggadocio** / brægə'dəusiəu / arrogant pretension — 15 **tall tale** a story that is difficult to believe — 21 **crescent** / kresnt / Halbmond — 22 **tidewater** low coastal land — 25 **to reap** to gather — 26 **influx** inflow — 28 **to top out** to be finished — 33 **mañana** Spanish for tomorrow — 35 **unencompassable** infinite — 35 **bonanza** / bəu'nænzə / something like a gold-mine or oil-well that is prospering greatly — 38 **gross national product** / grəus / Bruttosozialprodukt — 40 **GNP** = gross national product — 40 **per capita** for each person — 40 **hospitable** giving hospitality — 45 **to gear to** to direct at — 45 **entrepreneurial** / ɔntrəprə'njuəriəl / unternehmerisch — 45 **go-go** here: lively action — 47 **menial** servant — 52 **rugged** rough — 52 **heedless** not paying attention to s.th. — 52 **we ain't gonna reward** slang for: we are not going to reward — 53 **unreconstructed** not reconciled to political or social change — 55 **perky** boldly cheerful — 56 **git** Texan for get — 57 **flushed with** filled with — 59 **to topple** to fall down — 63 **veneer** / vi'niə / top layer

I. Question on the text

1. Give an outline of the whole text, showing the main structural elements. (Indicate line numbers where necessary.)
2. In the headline Texas is given the epithet "superstate". What factors helped to make Texas what it is now?
3. Look at the stylistic devices and the tone of the first and last paragraphs and explain their specific functions in the text. (Bear in mind that the whole article is addressed to an American audience.)
4. Explain the meaning of "the true-grit myth of the frontier" (line 13) and the "state of mind called Texas" (line 16).
5. Explain the following phrases in their context (with special regard to the italicized words):
   a) San Antonio — despite its *mañana philosophy* — is tenth (line 33).
   b) Texas's *rugged* but *heedless* individualism (lines 51—52).

6. Why can it be said that Texas is more hospitable to business than any other state in the Union (line 44)?
7. Paraphrase the following passages. Do not use the italicized words.
   a) a *god-awful won't-it-ever-end stretch* of *monotony* (line 3)
   b) In a state so *geared* to production and *old-fashioned entrepreneurial go-go* (line 45)
8. Which two main features are characteristic of the mode of presentation the author uses in this text?
9. In bringing home Texas's economic bigness to the reader the author uses a particular device. Which one and where?

II. Composition

Choose one of the following topics. Write about 200 words.
1. Write a critical letter to the state representative mentioned in line 52, commenting on his statement.
2. Write an ironic essay on the 'typical Texan' as he often appears in Western movies.

12 Parameters of communicology

In the nick of time the English are showing signs of rallying to the defense of their own language against the forces of corruption and nonsense. Such counterattacks, of course, are familiar enough in France, where the invasion of Franglais can be conveniently blamed on the Americans. And in Britain, too, the debasement is widely regarded as due to the Americanization of the language. But really the corruption comes from within, and is part of a more fundamental change in thinking — or not thinking. The English counterattack comes from several different quarters. The Times of London now prints periodic articles about the debasement of words. And a succession of writers have depicted the horrendous effects of the corruption of language on clarity. "We talk of parameter when we mean limit," wrote the historian Robert Skidelsky in the Spectator, "sanctions when we mean punishment, viable when we mean workable, managerial skills when we mean leadership . . . We say 'there are constraints on our freedom of action' rather than 'we can't do this'.
Part of this counterattack, no doubt, is only the latest stage in a long rearguard action to preserve the English language which has been losing

ground over the last two centuries. It is at least as old as Dr. Johnson, who began his great dictionary in 1747 with a belief that he could define the English language forever — and finished it eight years later realizing that the subject could never be settled. Grammarians and pedants, whether in Britain or America, will always resist the invasion of popular speech and will probably look rather silly a decade later.

When the great American critic Edmund Wilson visited Britain in 1946 he was upset to hear young Englishmen using phrases like 'OK' and 'that's right' or 'het up' which are now firmly installed in the language. Kingsley Amis has been crusading against the use of 'hopefully' to mean 'let us hope', a practice which has been creeping into Britain from America. But the new supplement to the Oxford English Dictionary has already betrayed the cause by including the new meaning, even though with the parenthetical note: "avoided by many writers."

The fact is that the English language is enriched as much as debased by American popular speech, and simple words like 'teach-in', 'breakdown', 'comeback', 'crack-up', 'bad-mouthing', 'breakthrough', or 'ripoff', all of which have now crossed the Atlantic, have a directness that is irresistible to writers as well as talkers. The fact that many of them are influenced by German words (like 'hoffentlich' or 'Durchbruch') is held against them by purists, but that only points to the roots that are common to both languages.

The weakness of the British opposition to such American imports is that there is no comparable flow of new words from Britain. George Orwell, complaining about Americanizations in 1944, wrote that "there is no chance of resisting the American influence unless we can put new life into English itself" and he blamed the stagnation of British English, like so much else, on the class system which made educated Englishmen reluctant to use working-class phrases: they preferred to use American slang, like "sez you" to a Cockney equivalent like "not alf."

It is true that many American phrases are longer than their old British equivalent: 'no way' simply means 'no', 'how come that' means 'why' and 'at this moment in time' means 'now'. But longwindedness is often very useful on television, to give one time to think.

The British, since they have rejected their own introvert past and the image of the strong, silent man, will naturally look to American as the language of extroversion.

But the real threat to the English language comes not from American colloquialism or from the ordinary people, but from the politicians, the company executives and, worst of all, from the academics themselves. It is the heavy, hollow jargon of sociological theses, bureaucratic instructions and political speeches that is the real nightmare, for it obscures the language of humanity and clear thought in an endless parade of mechanical nouns and and abstract concepts that can justify any kind of skulduggery, and that depicts human life as being part of an intricate and unchangeable machine.

This industrialization of the language became more evident with each new development of communications. Electricity, radio, television, computers and spacecraft all produced their own metallic vocabulary of 'feedbacks', 'contacts', 'images', 'inputs', 'processing', 'accelerators' or 'orbits' — a vocabulary which was rapidly extended to describe not only machines but people. And the more deadly practitioners of sociology, accountancy and social engineering encouraged still further the assumption that people were no different from cogs in machines with a new language of 'situations', 'model', 'systems'. The long nouns multiplied and clustered together, marching in phalanxes, protecting themselves with the passive tense to avoid any indulgence in words like 'I' and 'you'.

The English like to blame all this either on the Americans — or, even more improbably, on the Germans. The Germans, the English sometimes complain, having lost a fleeting eighteenth-century opportunity to take over the American language, are now Germanizing it from within by infusing it with the long nouns and abstractions they so deeply cherish. But Britain still has not launched an effective counterattack by providing the vigorous revival of the native and earthy language that Orwell longed for. And in the dehumanizing of language is a universal phenomenon: we are, in other words, all in it together, this ongoing process, this developmental matrix. We are all wired up, plugged in, switched on and ready for take-off into an orbit where we finally lose sight of human beings altogether.

1140 words Anthony Sampson in *Newsweek*, 1977.

Annotations

1 **parameter** / pə'ræmitə / here: limit — 1 **communicology** / kɔmjuni'kɔlədʒi science of communication — 2 **in the nick of time** just in time — 2 **to rally** to come to(gether) — 5 **Franglais** French word meaning a mixture of French and English (Français + Anglais) — 5 **convenient** suited to one's needs — 6 **debasement** corruption; decline — 11 **to depict** to describe — 11 **horrendous** terrible — 17 **rear-guard action** fight between an army in retreat and the enemy — 27 **het up** excited — 32 **parenthetical** / pærən'θetikəl / additional — 34 **teach-in** discussion of a subject of topical interest in a college, with students, staff and other speakers — 35 **crack-up** failure, breakdown — 35 **bad-mouthing** cursing — 35 **ripoff** an act of stealing — 48 **sez you** (Am) = not'alf (Brit) you

must be crazy — 53 **introvert** rather interested in one's own thoughts and feelings than in things outside — 55 **extroversion** the opposite of being introvert — 60 **nightmare** s.th. dreaded; strong fear — 63 **skulduggery** / skʌl'dʌgəri / clever deception — 63 **intricate** complicated — 70 **accountancy** Buchhaltung — 71 **social engineering** applied social science — 72 **cog** Zahnrad — 73 **to cluster together** to grow closely together — 74 **phalanx** a group that is fiercely active in support of some purpose — 75 **indulgence** giving way to — 78 **fleeting** quick-moving — 80 **to infuse** to fill — 82 **rigorous** very strong — 85 **matrix** / 'meitriks / mold — 85 **to wire up** to connect with wires — 85 **to plug in** to connect with an electric current G. einschalten — 86 **orbit** the path of a man-made object round the earth

I. Questions on the text

1. Summarize the main facts concerning the Americanization of the English language.
2. In the text several writers are mentioned who devoted themselves to the cause of the English language. Give their names and characterize their ideas resp. efforts.
3. Why is it justified to say that the British counterattack on Americanization comes "in the nick of time" (line 2)?
4. Where in his article does the author refer to and enlarge on the statement "But really the corruption comes from within" (line 7)? Interpret the relevant passage(s).
5. Why does the Times attack the debasement of the English language?
6. What view does the author hold on the influence of American on English and which factors does he mention that account for the advancement of Americanisms?
7. Explain lines 53—55 with special regard to the terms *introvert past* and *language of extroversion.*
8. What is meant by "industrialization of language" (line 65)?
9. Explain the contents of lines 76—80.
10. Paraphrase the following expressions. Do not use the italicized words.
    a) It is the *heavy, hollow* jargon of sociological theses . . . that is the real *nightmare* (lines 58—59).
    b) But Britain still has not *launched* an *effective* counterattack by providing the *vigorous revival* of the native and *earthy* language (lines 81—82).
11. Interpret the last sentence of the essay.
12. To delineate the influence of American English and the British reaction the author uses metaphors and phrases taken from a specialized field. Which one and which phrases? What is their effect in the text?

II. Composition

Choose one of the following topics. Write about 200 words.

1. Comment on the following statement by Talleyrand: "Man has been given language to hide his thoughts."
2. Write a letter to an English or American penfriend, commenting on your own experience with English language learning.

Lösungsvorschlag für Textaufgabe Nr. 8 "Dracula Lives"

I. Questions on the text

1. In the introduction (lines 2—8), the author enumerates Dracula's qualities and shortly describes his continued existence in the media. This does not only arouse the reader's interest, it also justifies the title of the article. The following little passage (lines 9—11), reminiscent of a concrete theatre scene, serves as a transition to the development of the Dracula myth in history, literature, and film.
After shortly mentioning Bram Stoker's novel, the author tells us about the belief in vampires in ancient Egypt and in parts of modern Greece. Subsequently, he gives us a short survey of the life and deeds of the historical Dracula (lines 18—25).
Then he returns to different film versions of Dracula, emphasizing Bela Lugosi's particular role in that field. This survey is concluded by an anecdote concerning Lugosi's funeral (lines 42—45).
The last part of the essay (lines 46—60) is introduced by a question asking for the potency of the Dracula myth. In the following two passages the writer gives us a psycho-analytical explanation of the main problems connected with the lasting popularity of that fictitious monster. The last line takes up the title phrase again — thus the wheel has come full circle.
2. The author does not mention Dracula by name, but only refers to him with the pronoun 'he'. In this way a certain tension is built up. The style is highly literary and even pretentious, in some traits almost archaic, thus recalling the atmosphere of a past century (e.g. aristocrat of evil).

Examples:	he sates himself on blood	(modern: satisfies)
	sanguine quest	(modern: quest for blood)
	lethal glamour	(modern: deadly glamour)

In addition, the writer makes use of effective rhythmic patterns and well-balanced antitheses. (He has died a thousand deaths ... and still his lethal glamour persists/deathless as our love of horror ... and our fear of death)

3. Both are notorious for their thirst for blood. Bram Stoker took the Wallachian setting for his novel.

4. There is extensive use of the famous vampire especially on the screen — as the long history of film version shows —, but as well on TV, in books, and theatre plays.

5. Dracula's popularity can be accounted for by the fact that a vampire is an ideal figure on the screen because he attracts people by his eeriness and his obvious immortality.

6. Lugosi was practically limited to roles in horror films, he became the prisoner of that literary figure.

7. This incident does not only reveal a special sense of black humor on the side of the two actors, it also shows that Lugosi could be taken for the figure he had impersonated so well.

8. Horror tales — or movies — are a particular type of fun. They give us vicarious excitement and suspense, transmuting our subliminal anxieties into clear-cut conflicts. At the same time we are reminded that the whole action is unreal and that we can enjoy the danger without being endangered ourselves.

9. The title is justified because the figure of Dracula is still alive in the media. Furthermore, according to the author's psychoanalytical interpretation, he lives on in ourselves.

10. a) his mortal/deadly enchantment/fascination/magic/spell continues/lives on/endures

b) a great escape that changes/transforms our formless/shapeless anxieties

II. Composition

The following essays have been written by students of a Leistungskurs.

1. Why do so many people like horror movies? Give arguments.

Coming home after a hard working-day to a comfortable place, having some hours to relax — that's what it could be. But curiously enough many people — and even after considerable stress at their work — prefer to go to the movies and to get some thrill. So, why are they doing that?

I suppose they have the urgent desire to be really moved, to feel some tremor in their bodies and to be reminded of the fact that there are still feelings in them, even if it is the feeling of being scared.

Maybe they have forgotten those happy feelings which can also move and give excitement, maybe they have become blunt and the only way of feeling some kind of sensitiveness is to be shocked.
But there could be another reason: absolute boredom. Perhaps people have lost their feelings by doing the very same things every day. Work may be repetitive, and what can we do with our spare time if we are tired or indolent? It's very easy to sit in a cinema and let all the pictures pass without doing anything.

2. Violence in horror movies and violence in westerns or whodunits — are they the same?

I think you can't compare violence in horror movies with violence in westerns and whodunits. In westerns and detective films all actors play human beings, whereas in horror films the hero is no normal person. He is a mixture of a ghost and a devil. Cruelties committed by him haven't such negative results on the behaviour of the spectator. He won't transfer the violence to his everyday life, because he is aware of the fact that Dracula and all his deeds are just an illusion. But if the spectator watches how normal men are injuring each other as it happens e.g. in a cowboy film, it is rather difficult for him not to react as aggressively himself in real life. There is more space for an identification with John Wayne and his behaviour than with a being that can fly and sucks blood. Everybody knows that horror tales and the violence shown in them have never happened. They are written just for fun, whereas the Wild West and our criminality were and are cruel reality.

3. Write a letter to an American or British friend who is keen on horror movies. You disagree with him on that point and give him an ironical reply.

Hi John,
You are well? I hope so. The time I'm writing you this letter would be right for you, it's about midnight. The full moon's rays fall on my bed and the shadows on the wall send shivers down my spine. Pressing the necklace with the cross to my breast I suddenly had to think of you. Really, and I laughed because it's funny, well, just crazy to think that a vampire should show up in that wonderful, romantic atmosphere which is so natural and has nothing to do with nightly fearful spook. I switched on the lights, took a sheet of paper and began to write. I hope you are not angry because I disagree with you and your fancy for horror movies. Films should be entertainment and horror movies fail at this point. In my

opinion, they frighten us, raise our blood-pressure and prevent us from sleeping.
I must confirm this: I couldn't sleep because I saw a Dracula movie. But I'll finish now, the smell of garlic's making me drowsy.
'Bye' for now.

987 654 32